Steam in South Wales

DEREK HUNTRISS | WITH PHOTOGRAPHY BY **ALAN JARVIS**

Ian Allan
PUBLISHING

First published 2013

ISBN 978 0 7110 3729 8

© Derek Huntriss 2013

Published by Ian Allan Publishing Ltd, Hersham, Surrey KT12 4RG

Printed in China

Visit the Ian Allan Publishing website at *www.ianallanpublishing.com*

Photographic credits
All the photographs in this book were taken by Alan Jarvis.

Acknowledgements
Sincere thanks are offered to Alan Jarvis for allowing unrestricted access to his colour collection for use in this title. In addition sincere thanks are given to Cornwall Railway Society member Mike Roach for the loan of numerous text books on the subject, without which the captions could not have been written.

Sincere thanks are offered to fellow members of the Welsh Railways Research Circle for their assistance, in particular to Ray Caston for sharing his in-depth knowledge.

FRONT COVER 0-6-0PT No 9488 is seen departing from Quakers Yard High Level with a Neath–Pontypool Road working on 16 May 1964. Beyond High Level station the line to Neath swung west, crossing the River Taff before entering the single-bore West Tunnel under Bryn Glas and into the Cynon Valley. Since that time the spoil tips above Bryn Glas have been re-profiled and reduced, and across the former Neath trackbed an expressway has been constructed along the west side of the valley.

TITLE PAGE Heading towards Walnut Tree Junction, a '56xx' 0-6-2T passes Penrhos Junction with a loaded coal train for Barry Docks on 27 August 1964. A visitor here today would see a very different scene. The cutting and road bridge have been filled in, with new houses appearing, the only identifying feature being the outline of Mynydd Machen in the distance.

BACK COVER In the western suburbs of Cardiff '72xx' 2-8-2T No 7250 is seen entering Ely (Main Line) station with an up loose-coupled freight train in August 1959. The sub-title 'Main Line' was added by the GWR in 1924, presumably to indicate the location of the station, although there was no passenger station on the former Taff Vale Railway. The previous title had been 'Ely for Llandaff'. At that time the old carriage on the end of the platform was in use as a classroom for the Mutual Improvement Association.

Introduction

It was May 1962 when the author felt very disappointed at missing a local railway society's trip to visit the steam motive power depots in South Wales. Having just completed his GCE exams and with no more school work, he jumped on his bicycle, travelling around many steam depots in South Wales as far as Llanelly from his home in Coventry. What this keen enthusiast had failed to grasp was that on weekdays most engines were busy earning their keep, unlike on Sundays when most society visits were made and the engines were 'on shed'. However, all was not lost. At this point in time another enthusiast based in Cardiff was busy recording the local scene on Kodachrome film for us to enjoy many years later. His name is Alan Jarvis.

Alan was born in Cardiff in 1931 and has lived there ever since. His railway photography began in 1948 and since that date he has amassed a collection of some 16,000 black-and-white negatives and colour transparencies covering operations both in the UK and abroad. With the help of a string of motor cycles, Alan has been able to record activities not only in his native Glamorgan but also other parts of South Wales which he has shared with us in this book. The book first takes the reader to West Wales before visiting Swansea and heading through Llandovery to Sugar Loaf Summit. A journey along the former Newport & Brecon line gets us back to the English border with visits to Chepstow and Severn Tunnel. From here the reader is taken back across the valleys in a generally westerly direction before arriving back in Swansea.

The story of railways in South Wales, their history and operations has been told in hard statistics, of lines opened, companies founded, dates of openings, stock owned and coal carried. The valleys were richly blessed with the minerals that were the basis of Britain's industrial growth and one-time world leadership. Of paramount importance were the operational practices that had to be introduced to cope with this traffic and which were honed for over a century. To cope with the sudden demands for traffic in addition to those of a daily nature, sophisticated control methods had to be put in place. Demands for traffic to be moved in the valleys could occur anywhere, these being compounded by the geographical nature of the valleys precluding the construction of coal holding sidings at the mines to buffer the fluctuations.

The railways in the valleys were responsible for the relative ease with which immigrants could arrive, it being a rather surprising fact that immigration from England was second only to emigration to the United States. For many years the railways were also the only means of leaving the valleys for the seaside; with expectations not being as great as today, day trips to Barry Island or the Gower were the high spot of the year. Railway staff would be worked off their feet on Bank Holidays as every available locomotive and coach was pressed into traffic. Often station layouts had restricted accommodation, so frequency had to be increased to cope with demand.

Today times have changed, and the need for both freight and excursion traffic has now largely disappeared. But before films fade and documents disappear, we can experience a glimpse into times past which are fast disappearing into history.

Derek Huntriss
Coventry
November 2012

Bibliography

Paul Bolger: *BR Steam Motive Power Depots: WR* (Ian Allan Publishing)
Denis Dunstone: *Welsh Railways – A Photographer's View* (Gomer Press)
Don Gatehouse and Geoff Dowling: *British Railways Past and Present: South Wales, Part 1* (Past & Present Publishing)
Terry Gough: *British Railways Past and Present: South Wales, Part 3* (Past & Present Publishing)
Michael Hale: *Steam in South Wales* Vols 1-4 (Oxford Publishing Co)
Michael Hale: *Steam in South Wales* Vols 5 and 6 (Welsh Railways Research Circle)
John Hutton: *Taff Vale Railway Miscellany* (Oxford Publishing Co)
Gwyn Briwant Jones and Denis Dunstone: *The Vale of Neath Line – Neath to Pontypool Rd* (Gomer Press)
Brian J. Miller: *Rickard's Record: Cardiff and the Valleys* Vols 1 and 2 (The Wider View)
Vic Mitchell and Keith Smith: *Country Railway Routes: Brecon to Newport* (Middleton Press)
Vic Mitchell and Keith Smith: *Welsh Valleys: Mountain Ash to Neath* (Middleton Press)
Vic Mitchell and Keith Smith: *Welsh Valleys: Pontypool to Mountain Ash* (Middleton Press)
James Page: *Railways in the Valleys* (Guild Publishing)
Nigel Welbourn: *Lost Lines: Wales* (Ian Allan Publishing)
Ian L. Wright: *Branch Line Byways: South Wales* (Atlantic Transport Publishing)

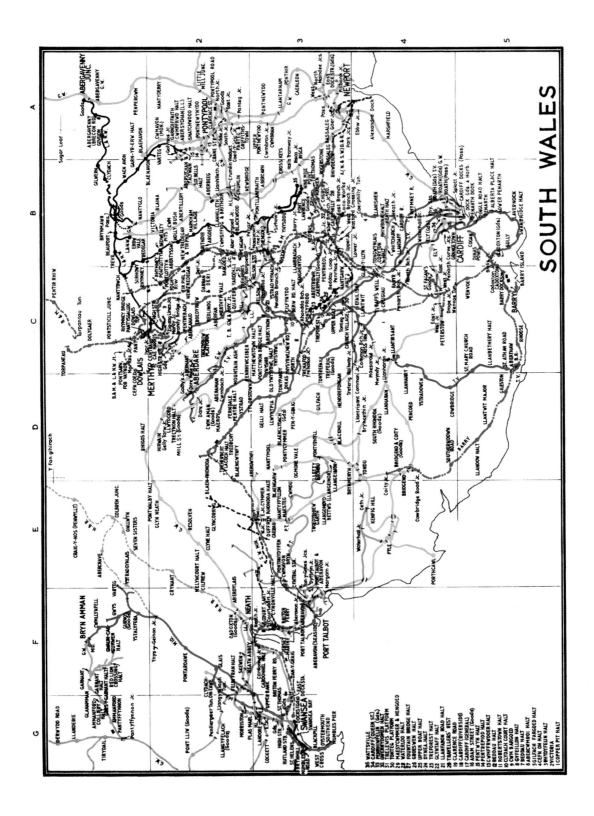

This view taken at Fishguard Harbour station on 6 September 1962 depicts 0-6-0PT No 9602 about to depart with a train for Clarbeston Road. Space to build the station on this site was achieved by blasting away the cliff face and using the rubble to create new land from the sea. The locomotive depot at Fishguard was sometimes called Goodwick and was coded FGD by the GWR and later 87J by BR. It had an allocation of about 15 locomotives which rarely travelled far from home. It closed one year after this picture was taken in September 1963, its allocation being scattered between Duffryn Yard, Old Oak Common, Oxford and Pontypool Road.

LEFT Having taken the train depicted in the previous picture, the photographer captured this cameo view of No 9602 taking water at Clarbeston Road station. With the main line running to Whitland, the station nameboard read 'Clarbeston Road – Junction for Fishguard'. This connecting service had once been provided by '14xx' 0-4-2Ts working auto-trains, but these had departed some years earlier. Before the arrival of the railway Clarbeston Road didn't exist – it was simply a cluster of thatched cottages and a pub on a lonely crossroads north of Wiston. It was only after the arrival of the railway in the 1850s that the name was introduced, despite the fact it was nowhere near Clarbeston village – the village expanding rapidly thereafter.

ABOVE This detailed view taken at Rhydowen on 16 June 1962 shows the end of a Hawksworth Brake Third coach as it forms the 11.35am from Whitland to Cardigan hauled by 0-6-0PT No 1666. This little branch was authorised in 1869 and linked the slate quarries at Glogue with the South Wales main line at Whitland. Crossing the eastern end of the Prescelly Hills, the line was severely graded, climbing northwards to the summit at Crymmych Arms at the head of the Taf valley.

Having descended the 1 in 40 into the classic branch line terminus at Cardigan, No 1666 is
seen propelling its train out of the platform. With only one year of operation left before closure,
the station appears quite busy with a '45xx' 2-6-2T simmering outside the sub-shed.

A minor mishap occurred at Pontarddulais on the Graig Merthyr colliery system on 25 March
1963, when Andrew Barclay 0-4-0T No 1073/06 left the rails during shunting operations.
In this view lifting jacks are being put in place with the locomotive soon to return to action.

Probably the single most photographed locomotive allocated to Swansea East Dock Motive Power Depot (MPD), former Cardiff Railway 0-4-0ST No 1338 is captured on 26 April 1963. Built by Kitson & Co in 1898, the locomotive acquired the number 1338 when absorbed into the GWR. It subsequently had a somewhat chequered career, spending part of World War 2 at Stewarts & Lloyds steelworks at Landore, and was used for shunting at Bridgwater Docks in Somerset. In 1960 it was allocated to Swansea East Dock, where it was used for shunting certain low-level lines around the South Dock until withdrawn in September 1963, when it was the sole survivor of the GWR standard-gauge constituent engines. It is now operational at Didcot Railway Centre.

STEAM IN SOUTH WALES

Also on 26 April 1963, a visit to Swansea Victoria sees some lively action as BR Standard 2-6-4T No 80099 leaves with a local train, whilst the driver of 0-6-0PT No 3604 sportingly agrees to move his empty coaches a few yards at the same time.

The LNWR's terminus at Swansea Victoria was certainly more imposing that its Midland Railway counterpart, although the roof which was damaged during World War 2 was never repaired, the station seeing its last passenger train on 15 June 1964.

This general view of the former London & North Western Railway's sub-shed at Llandovery was taken on 16 May 1964. Situated to the south of Llandovery station on the east side of the line, the LNWR's first construction on this site was opened on 8 October 1868, and consisted of a three-track straight dead-ended shed that had been previously built for use at Llandrindod Wells. Facilities included a 42ft turntable and a ramped coal stage with water tank above. By 1900 this building was derelict and was closed, being replaced in 1901 by a new four-track straight dead-ended shed with a northlight-pattern slate roof, after which the first shed was demolished. Locomotive operations ceased on 10 August 1964, although the shed building stood until demolished in 1978.

Also seen on 16 May 1964 was this unidentified Stanier '8F' 2-8-0 passing Sugar Loaf Summit with a southbound freight. The signalbox at Sugar Loaf Summit was of LNWR Type 4 design, having an 18-lever frame, and was situated by the up line just north of the 1,001yd Sugar Loaf Tunnel, between Llanwrtyd Wells and Llandovery No 1 signalboxes. In this view it is carrying a post-1935 design nameboard. The box closed on 3 October 1965

ABOVE Here we see 0-6-0PT No 4621 waiting to leave Brecon with a service to Neath on 23 June 1962. All passenger services on this route were withdrawn some four months later in October 1962, leaving only freight services. No subway or footbridge was ever provided here, passengers using the unsupervised crossing which can be seen in the foreground of this picture.

RIGHT Climbing continuously for 3 miles at 1 in 38 before reaching Pentir Rhiw with a Brecon-Newport train, 0-6-0PT No 8766 is standing at the north end of the loop on 13 May 1959. To the right the runaway refuge siding goes to a point beyond the cottage which is just visible behind the train. The gentleman seen filling the tank is a former Newport driver, and although retired from railway service he was enjoying his trip in an unofficial capacity.

South of Pentir Rhiw the passenger was taken over what was one of the most breathtaking rail journeys in Britain. This picture taken on 13 May 1959 depicts two 0-6-0PTs at Torpantau station with a northbound ammonia tank train. These trains originated at the ICI chemical works at Dowlais, where they were loaded with ammonia, then routed through Torpantau to Talyllyn Junction and on to Hereford via Three Cocks Junction before forwarding to their final destination at Haverton Hill, Billingham. Whilst the station at Torpantau didn't open with the line, sidings for banking engines were provided from the outset.

0-6-0PT No 8766 is seen again on 13 May 1959, this time having arrived at Torpantau. The careful observer will spot that the signalbox has a slate-hung gable end – a necessary protection in a hostile environment. At 1,313ft above sea level Torpantau was one of Britain's loneliest railway locations; five minutes' walk away to the flanks of the Beacons the train would appear as a tiny speck in the landscape. It could be compared with Slochd (1,315ft) on the Highland main line; the 666yd Torpantau Tunnel had the distinction of being Britain's highest railway tunnel, being best remembered for its breathtaking eastern exit. Out of its inky blackness the marvellous panorama of Glyn Collwng appeared far below.

LEFT A picture taken on 2 June 1962 at Pontsticill Junction depicts '57xx' 0-6-0PT No 4635 with a train of empty ammonia tanks for Dowlais. Rail still exists here in the form of Rheillffordd Mynydd Brycheiniog, the narrow-gauge Brecon Mountain Railway, which was opened in 1980 along the former Brecon & Merthyr Railway trackbed from Pant. Built at Swindon in December 1942, No 4635 survived in traffic until July 1966, when it was withdrawn from Tyseley; it was scrapped that November by Garnham, Arris & Elton of Chesterfield.

ABOVE On every available summer evening in 1962 Alan kick-started his BSA 250cc motor bike into action to capture on film the 7.7pm from Newport to Brecon at as many locations as possible. Here he has captured the train at Fleur-de-lis on 30 June. Perched on the banks of the Rhymney river, Fleur-de-lis is a small village close to the town of Blackwood, near Caerphilly. Known locally as 'The Flower', the station was opened on 29 March 1926 and the platform was situated immediately to the north of the brewery siding.

LEFT Another view of the same train is taken this time at Bedwas station on 3 July 1962 with 0-6-0 No 2218 in charge. Some of the original signalboxes and equipment on the Brecon & Merthyr line were installed by Saxby & Farmer, which later merged with McKenzie & Holland. As can be seen in the example behind the train, somersault signals were the order of the day. Bedwas, situated two miles north-east of Caerphilly, was traditionally a farming community but owed much of its development to the South Wales coalfield and the Welsh coalmining industry. The nearby Bedwas Navigation Colliery had been completed by 1913 (the village growing from 2,080 souls in 1901 to 10,380 in 1961) and was closed in the miners' strike of 1984/5 and did not reopen.

ABOVE The 7.7pm from Newport to Brecon is featured once again in the charge of 0-6-0 No 2218 and is seen arriving at Trethomas. Opening in 1915, facilities at Trethomas were less substantial than those of the earlier stations on the line. Passenger services to Brecon and those to New Tredegar were withdrawn from 31 December 1962, the goods yard at Trethomas remaining open until 16 July 1964.

ABOVE This timeless scene taken at Chepstow depicts 0-6-0PT No 6426 about to depart with an auto-train for Newport on 30 August 1960. Behind the far platform can be seen Brunel's tubular bridge over the River Wye. Built in 1852, despite its appearance it was considered one of Brunel's major achievements and proved to be the prototype for his Royal Albert Bridge at Saltash. Following the lower part of the scenic Wye Valley between Chepstow and Monmouth, the 15-mile Wye Valley Railway was opened on 1 November 1876. Financially unsuccessful, it amalgamated in 1905 with the Great Western Railway until the railways were nationalised under the terms of the Transport Act 1947. Serving various metal works, paper mills and limestone quarries, the line was intended for use by goods traffic but also tourists, notably those visiting Tintern Abbey.

RIGHT The GWR main line enters Wales below ground using the Severn Tunnel. Here we see '51xx' 2-6-2T No 5110 piloting a BR Standard '9F' 2-10-0 with an eastbound coal train in April 1960. The 2-6-2T is carrying the target 'T3', one of 13 target numbers allocated to locomotives engaged on pilot duties through the tunnel. This train is leaving No 1 up loop for the journey through the tunnel. During World War 2 two loops were necessary to hold trains until a path could be found. This allowed more urgent traffic to pass. Construction of the 7,666yd tunnel began in 1873, some 3,600 men being employed on the site before its opening to traffic in 1886.

In this 1961 picture taken at Bishton the fireman of '72xx' 2-8-2T No 7252 can be seen levelling the coal in the bunker as it heads a coal train on the up relief line. Still in operation today at what is now known as Bishton Crossing, the level-crossing gates control the road traffic that passes over the railway line at this point. There is a small road tunnel beneath the track, but this is so low that many modern cars are too tall to pass through it.

Some two years later on 17 August 1963 No 7252 is seen again, this time leaving Newport Ebbw Junction (86A) locomotive shed. One month earlier No 7252 had been reallocated from Cardiff Radyr (88B) to Duffryn Yard (87B) MPD and was finally withdrawn from Severn Tunnel Junction (86E) in June 1965. After three months in store at that depot it was taken to the Steel Supply Co at Briton Ferry then resold to Cohen's yard at Morriston, Swansea, where it was broken up in May 1966.

Newport Pill (86B) MPD's 2-8-0T No 5256 is seen near St Brides with down coal empties on 9 June 1962. Behind the locomotive can be seen the Newport Transporter Bridge. Arguably the finest of its kind, its towers standing 645ft apart and rising 242ft above road level, it is electrically powered, the gondola being pulled across by a cable wound around a drum in the motor house on the east bank.

During the early 1960s traffic flows through the station at Newport High Street were altered to accommodate the additional movements of steel traffic and iron ore being shipped to and from the recently opened steelworks at Llanwern. Passenger and freight trains were segregated, with most down passenger trains being moved to the north side platforms, allowing clear paths for freight trains. Heading west, 2-8-0 No 2872 is using the down through line as it passes through the station on 15 May 1963 with a rake of unfitted open wagons. The coach in the background with the awning is advertising fishing tackle and air guns.

Severn Tunnel Junction (86E) MPD's 2-6-0 No 7322 prepares to leave Newport High Street for Cardiff on 18 May 1959. The '43xx' Moguls were the maids of all work on the GWR and had earned a reputation of being able to handle most types of traffic. The batch of locomotives renumbered 7322-41 between 1956 and 1959 were originally Collett locomotives numbered 9300-19 and were modified back to light buffer-beam design, No 7322 being given its new number in April 1957. After allocations to Aberdare (88J) and Gloucester Horton Road (85B) it was withdrawn in November 1961, being broken up at Swindon Works.

This 8 June 1963 picture shows BR Standard '9F' 2-10-0 No 92216 near Bassaleg with an up freight. There were two stations at Bassaleg, one on the former Brecon & Merthyr Railway and the other on the Western Valleys line. The section from Park Junction to Bassaleg ran over the lands of Sir Charles Morgan. From tramway days he was entitled to levy tolls on the traffic over his lands, until bought out by the GWR in the 1920s.

An interloper from the London Midland Region is seen near Rumney River Bridge, as Saltley (21A) MPD's Stanier '8F' No 48109 heads an up fitted van train on 22 April 1963.

Whilst the river is the Rhymney, the nearby residential area is known as Rumney. In the background can be seen the cooling towers of Roath power station, which were demolished in 1972.

Just over one month later, another view taken from the same vantage point features 'Hall' 4-6-0 No 6936 *Breccles Hall* with a Cardiff-Paignton train on 25 May 1963. The locomotive took its name from a property near Thetford which was begun by John Wodehouse and completed by his son Francis in 1583. The house and grounds later fell into disrepair, and the building became a farmhouse in the 19th century, later renovated by Arts & Crafts architect Detmar Blow.

A shunter sets the points for 0-6-2T No 5620 as it returns from propelling loaded coal wagons on the coaling stage at Cardiff East Dock (88L) MPD on 31 March 1963. At one time the Cardiff Docks area was served by several workshops and running sheds, but only East Dock survived into the 1930s. The GWR demolished the former Rhymney Railway workshops in 1931 and used the site for a new running shed. Under the GWR it was coded CED, becoming in BR days 88B, then 88L, and finally 88A.

This superb picture taken in Cardiff Docks at North East Junction sees 0-6-2T No 6632 propelling a rake of hoppers on 22 April 1963. No 6632 carries the target number H14, the 6.15am ex Radyr Junction, 'as ordered by control'. Coal exports from Cardiff Docks, which had been developed by John Crichton-Stuart, 2nd Marquis of Bute, peaked in 1913, when 10,700,000 tons were shipped, making Cardiff the biggest coal-exporting dock in the world. However, capacity issues, in terms of both siding and dock space, led to the development of Penarth, Newport and Barry docks as competitors for the lucrative South Wales coal trade.

Another view at Cardiff East Dock, this time depicting 'Castle' 4-6-0 No 5042 *Winchester Castle* and 0-6-0PT No 8484 in the shed yard on 2 July 1964. The shed first closed to steam in March 1958 when its shunting turns were dieselised, but when Cardiff Canton MPD was closed for conversion into a diesel depot it then had tender locomotives on its allocation, the second and final closure being from 2 August 1965.

2-8-0T No 5202 captured at East Dock on the same day. No 5202 had been reallocated from Duffryn Yard (87B) MPD to Cardiff East Dock in March of that year and survived until June 1965 before withdrawn. After storage at Steel Supply Co at Briton Ferry, it was resold to Cohen's yard at Morriston, Swansea, where it was broken up in June 1966.

Recorded in 1961, this general view of Cardiff Canton (then 88A)
features ex-works 'WD' 2-8-0 No 90069, one of the depot's
stud of these locomotives. Opened in June 1882, Canton was
one of the largest depots in Wales, with 120 or more
locomotives stabled there.

In another general view of the front yard at Cardiff Canton taken in 1961; the footbridge spanning the shed yard is clearly visible. In the words of the photographer, 'Canton was and still is a gathering point for enthusiasts far and wide, its great attraction being its easy visibility from a footbridge in De Croche Place, off Ninian Park Road. Until the premises were converted to a diesel depot, the footbridge, which now only crosses the main lines, extended across the full width of the shed and yard, the unwritten rule being that enthusiasts are tolerated as long as they remain on the footbridge. In its last years as a steam depot a few privileged folk were given the run of the place on the understanding that they behaved responsibly.'

'King' 4-6-0 No 6029 *King Edward VIII* prepares to leave Canton MPD on 23 February 1962. Originally named *King Stephen*, the locomotive carried its new identity from May 1936. The 'Kings' were not permitted to enter Cardiff until 1952 due to their 22$\frac{1}{2}$-ton axle loading. From that year they were permitted to work into Cardiff but with a severe speed restriction over Rumney River Bridge – though they rarely appeared. In 1958/9 the bridge was strengthened, allowing the locomotives through to Cardiff without restriction. Following dieselisation of passenger services to the West of England surplus 'Kings' were transferred to Cardiff Canton at the end of August 1960 to work through trains to London. Unfortunately their reign was short lived, all disappearing by the end of 1962.

Another superb line-up of motive power in the front yard at Cardiff Canton MPD, in April 1962, with 'King' 4-6-0 No 6018 *King Henry VI* in the foreground. It was sometimes thought mistakenly that the 'Kings' were too wide for the platforms at Cardiff General station, but when Nos 6023 and 6024 were towed to Dai Woodham's scrapyard in Barry they did indeed come into contact with the platform edges when passing through Cogan station, dislodging several slabs.

An exceptional rear three-quarter portrait of Cardiff Canton MPD's 'Modified Hall' 4-6-0 No 7913 *Little Wyrley Hall* as it leaves the depot past the old coaling stage in November 1960. No 7913 was to remain allocated to depots in South Wales until withdrawn from Severn Tunnel Junction (86E) MPD in March 1965. The locomotive was named after the hall of that name near Norton Canes in Staffordshire, the house being acquired by the Fowkes family during the reign of Elizabeth I and then by descent to the present-day Wallaces. The survival of this property was a 'miner' miracle as colliery workings encroached to within a few hundred feet of the east side of the house.

Locomotives receiving repairs at Caerphilly Works usually paid a visit to Canton MPD *en route* to their home shed. Here Reading (81D) MPD's 2-6-2T No 6119 is depicted in August 1961. In this photograph it is apparent that at some point the north-light roof of the shed has been raised, thought to be in 1925. No 6119 was to remain at that depot until withdrawn in May 1963 when it was taken to Swindon Works for scrapping.

Another example of fine workmanship at Caerphilly, this time in the form of Collett '2251' 0-6-0 No 2241 which gleams in the sun outside its home depot at Canton on an April day in 1961. Having closed to steam in September 1962, Canton was officially opened in September 1964 as a diesel depot employing nearly one hundred men, engaged primarily in heavy maintenance and servicing. It has since reopened in different ownership.

Waiting in the queue for coaling at Canton MPD, another Collett 0-6-0, No 2253, is seen in 1961. This locomotive has also been repaired at Caerphilly Works and will return to its home depot at Gloucester Horton Road (85B). Introduced from 1930, the '2251s' were replacements for the earlier 'Dean Goods' 0-6-0s.

Sharing many dimensions with the 'Dean Goods', they had increased boiler pressure and heating surface, giving a useful increase in power. These were the first GWR 0-6-0s to use the standard No 10 boiler as later fitted to the '94xx' and '15xx' locomotives.

With the Milk & Fish depot on the horizon in the background, 'Hall' 4-6-0 No 6939 *Calveley Hall* is seen in front of the straight shed in this November 1960 picture. With the labour shortages of the 1950s and '60s many steam locomotives were deplorably filthy, but several locomotive sheds, especially on the Western Region, made a point of keeping a small stud of main-line engines in 'showroom condition'. With the sunlight reflected on the polished paintwork, and with the shine on the burnished brass and copper, the locomotive's splendid appearance is a credit to the cleaners of Cardiff Canton MPD where this locomotive was allocated.

This final look at the front yard at Canton taken on 27 July 1962 includes the now-preserved 'Castle' 4-6-0 No 5043 *Earl of Mount Edgcumbe*. Having received its last heavy overhaul at Swindon in February of that year, it was allocated to Cardiff Canton in April. Continuing in service at Canton until it closed, it was then transferred to East Dock, where it stayed until withdrawn in December 1963. Stored until the following spring, it was then moved to Barry Docks, where it stayed until purchased by 7029 Clun Castle Ltd as a source of spares. Over the ensuing years Tyseley had developed the skills to undertake a massive restoration project, and a study into the feasibility of restoring the locomotive to main-line condition was undertaken. The project was given the go-ahead in 1996, the work finally being completed in 2008.

Hunslet Engine Co No 3787, built in 1953, is seen operating as NCB No 2 at Nantgarw Colliery on 8 September 1963. Opened in 1911, the colliery at Nantgarw boasted two large shafts and, at a depth of 2,568ft, was the deepest mine in south Wales. Despite being an outstanding example of the modern clean and efficient coal industry it was abandoned in 1927 due to a lack of manpower and to its being located above very complex geology. After reopening in 1937, and closing again when war broke out, the mine survived various pit closures until it finally succumbed after the 1984/5 miners' strike.

A view taken near Radyr station on 22 April 1963 shows a '56xx' 0-6-2T with a rake of empties. Until December 1957 Radyr was an uncoded sub-shed of Cardiff Cathays; during that month it was given the code 88A following the transfer of most of the locomotives from Cathays. On 1 January 1961 it was renumbered 88B, a code it retained until closure to steam on 26 July 1965.

Also seen on 22 April 1963 was 0-6-0PT No 3681 as it hurried through Radyr station with a brake van, the train, with hand-written target number H31, being the 1.45pm ex Radyr Junction, 'as ordered by control'. Seen clearly in the background, the signalbox was installed between 3 and 11 June 1961. A design dating from 1957, it had briefly stood at Swindon East in 1959 but had never been brought into use. The lever frame was, as standard by this time for the Western Region, a vertical-tappet five-bar GWR-type frame of 107 levers, positioned at the rear of the signalbox, giving signalmen a much clearer view of operations.

Another photograph taken at Radyr station on 22 April 1963 shows 0-6-2T No 6643 with a coal train on the down relief line, the target number 'J24' denoting the return leg of the 6.35am MX Barry Docks-Tymawr Colliery (near Pontypridd). The majority of Radyr MPD's steam allocation comprised '56xx' 0-6-2Ts, in addition to 0-6-0PTs and a small number of 2-8-2Ts which were used for the longer-distance turns. Having hauled the Monmouthshire Railway Society's 'Rambling 56' railtour on 31 July 1965, No 6643 was reallocated in the same month from Barry (88C) MPD to Llanelly (87F) MPD, where it remained until withdrawn in August. After one month in store at Llanelly the locomotive was broken up at Birds at Bynea.

A general view of the depot at Radyr taken on 5 May 1963 features 0-6-2Ts Nos 6656, 6614 and 6603 in the front yard. Situated a few miles outside Cardiff, the depot at Radyr supplied engines for freight and shunting duties, extensive sidings having been constructed for the reception of coal trains and formation of trains of empties. In 1887 a new line was opened to the Roath Dock, on the south-east side of the city, leaving the Taff Vale main line south of Radyr at Roath Branch Junction and crossing the eastern suburbs of Cardiff partly on an elevated section.

Probably the single most distinguished visitor to Radyr shed came on 18 March 1964 when ex-LNER Class A3 Pacific No 4472 *Flying Scotsman* arrived with a Festiniog Railway Society special from Doncaster to Cardiff. It had conveyed its owner, Alan Pegler, and marked the occasion when he received an award for services to tourism in Wales. During the presentation the locomotive was taken to Radyr, where it was serviced with coal and water, and is seen here receiving attention inside the shed.

With a full head of steam 0-6-0PT No 6435 is seen racing through Penarth Dock station in March 1960 as it takes a run at the 1 in 49 of Dingle Bank with auto-train 'JB'. This train passed through this station some 12 times during the course of a working day but stopped only once, four minutes after its departure from Penarth with the 12.23pm service from Cardiff. Serving the locality in west Cardiff, this train operated between Pontypridd, the Barry main line, St Fagans, Cardiff and Coryton, running over lines formerly owned by the GWR, the Barry Railway, the Taff Vale Railway, the Rhymney Railway and the Cardiff Railway.

Another view of auto-train 'JB' is taken this time from the window of Leckwith Junction signalbox in April 1960. 'JB' has the Ely distant at clear and will have a quick run down the main line towards Ely station, the box-to-box bell code for this train down the main line being 5-pause-1. It started its weekday journeys at Pontypridd, motive power being provided by Abercynon shed. Seemingly exclusive to South Wales, a 'target' system of train identification was used and took the form of a disc affixed to the front of the locomotive. This was inherited from pre-Grouping times, and for this train the letter 'J' denoted Abercynon shed, with the sub-letter 'B'.

ABOVE Auto-train 'JB' is captured once again from the window of Leckwith Junction signalbox in April 1960 as it heads towards Ely. The tracks coming in from the left connected to the former Taff Vale Railway to Radyr via Waterhall. Nominally a freight-only line, it was also used for football specials from the west to Ninian Park Halt. Auto-trains were a firm favourite of the photographer who initially captured these workings on black-and-white film, but towards the end of their days in 1960 he captured them on colour film at many locations.

RIGHT The abutments of the former Barry Railway viaduct are visible behind this 0-6-0 pannier tank as it heads westwards from St Fagans with a rake of steel wagons on 12 April 1963. The unusual signal in the foreground has holes in its arm, and controlled the reversing of trains from the down main line into a running loop which had commenced at St Fagans.

With the locomotive's reporting disc clearly visible in this August 1959 picture the fireman of 0-6-0PT No 6438 leans out of the cab window to collect (from its trackside holder) the token authorising the train to proceed to the single-line section which led up to the Barry main line at Tyn-y-Caeau Junction.

The station building at St Fagans was an original South Wales Railway structure, having been built in 1872, but despite the National Museum of Wales' presence at nearby St Fagans Castle it was demolished soon after the station closed in September 1962, the museum showing no interest.

Once again auto-train 'JB' is captured at St Fagans, this time in the hands of 0-6-0PT No 6435 as it propels its train towards Cardiff in June 1960. Whilst the lamp below the chimney would appear to be in the wrong place, it will be correct as a 'stopping passenger train' when running in the opposite direction. Transferred to St Blazey (83E) in November 1963 and withdrawn in October 1964, No 6435 covered more than 570,000 miles in service. Together with 0-6-0PTs Nos 6412 and 6430 the engine was purchased by the Dart Valley Railway, initially to operate on the Buckfastleigh-Totnes branch in Devon and subsequently on the Paignton-Kingswear line. In July 2008 it was purchased from the DVLR by the Bodmin & Wenford Railway.

ABOVE A '42xx' 2-8-0T is seen near the hamlet of St Georges with an up iron ore train on 12 April 1963, the arches of the viaduct carrying the former Barry Railway being clearly visible in the background. Formed in 1884, the Barry Docks & Railway Co provided alternatives to the Cardiff Docks and the railways that served them. The main line from Hafod and Treforest junctions down to Barry Docks was officially opened on 18 July 1889, when coal traffic began to flow, amounting to one million tons in that year. By 1891 the company name was changed to the Barry Railway, running powers being obtained over the TVR to the Rhymney Railway at Walnut Tree Junction.

RIGHT '43xx' 2-6-0 No 6369 hurries a down Porthcawl train through St Fagans station on 17 June 1962. The highest signal on the gantry controlled the down main line, and the left-hand arm entry to the down running loop. The right-hand arm indicated entry to the branch. The empty 'doll' had once carried an arm allowing entry to the branch and thence to the Barry Railway/GWR exchange sidings.

Seen in afternoon sunshine on 21 July 1962, 2-8-0T No 5234 has passed through Plymouth Woods with an up coal train and is approaching Ely (Main Line) station. The stations at Ely and St Fagans were closed to passengers from 10 September 1962, when the Pontypridd auto-train service was withdrawn. A Newport Ebbw Junction (86A) locomotive for much of its working life, No 5234 was withdrawn in June 1963, when it was stored until April 1964, being broken up by Hayes of Bridgend the following month.

This splendid picture, taken in winter light near Llandow, on the former Barry Railway from Barry to Bridgend, in January 1961, depicts an 0-6-2T with a ballast train passing a somersault signal. Signalling on the lines of the former Barry Railway was provided by Saxby & Farmer or a subsidiary, Evans O'Donnell, whose finials were different from those on the McKenzie & Holland posts found on many other South Wales lines.

This general view shows the platforms and signalbox of the former Barry Railway station at Llandow Halt in January 1961. The signalbox at Llandow was sited on top of the cutting for better observation of traffic. The signal wires were required to pass around two sets of pulley wheels with the point rodding having to change direction twice. On top of the embankment on the left can be seen a typical Barry Railway somersault signal, its additional height allowing better sighting by drivers of approaching trains.

Another view on the former Barry Railway line to Bridgend, this time taken from a moving train passing Pant Mawr quarry in July 1961, depicts 0-6-0PT No 3690 with a rake of loaded limestone wagons. The underlying rock in this area is a conglomerate limestone which is porous and absorbs surface water through fissures and cracks, and is believed to have been exploited since Roman times. With only two quarries remaining in operation, the area continues to supply lime for the steelworks at Port Talbot.

A few days before the closure of this line on 12 April 1963, 0-6-2T No 5691 is seen with a loaded coal train bound probably for the power station at Aberthaw. To arrive at this point the train had crossed two vidaucts, one over the GWR main line and connecting chord to the Barry at Tyn-y-Caeau Junction, the other over the River Ely. The chimney to the left of the signalbox was all that remained of the Barry Railway pumping station which lifted water from the river, supplying a large water tank and water columns nearby.

After taking the previous picture the photographer quickly took this attractive rear three-quarter view depicting the train shortly before entering the 1,867yd Wenvoe Tunnel. Following the line's closure the tunnel was used by the local water authority to carry a large-diameter water main carrying additional supplies to the Barry area. Treherbert (88F) MPD's No 5691 was subsequently reallocated to Tondu (88H) in February 1963, before allocation in November 1964 to Radyr (88B) MPD, where it remained in service until withdrawn in June 1965.

Visible from the churchyard at Porthkerry, this view recorded on 19 May 1964 features a coal train being worked over the viaduct by an 0-6-2T assisted at the rear by another member of the class. This viaduct was the principal structure on the Vale of Glamorgan section of the Barry Railway and, unlike most of the infrastructure on the railway, was poorly constructed, partially collapsing twice while under construction in 1896 and again six weeks after the line was opened in 1898. A tortuous deviation had to be built before full traffic recommenced over the viaduct in April 1900.

One of 10 members of this class allocated to Barry (88C) MPD, BR Standard Type 3 2-6-2T No 82042 passes the signalbox at Rhoose with an up rake of coal empties in September 1960. The whole of the Barry Railway, including the docks, became a constituent part of the Great Western Railway in 1923. Local traffic on the line included that from the limestone quarries and the cement works at Aberthaw, and Rhoose cement works at the eastern end of the line. Wartime traffic was created from Tremains and Brackla Hill at Bridgend and the RAF base at St Athan. The docks were separated from the railway in 1961 as part of the British Docks Board. Traffic has increased since the full opening of Aberthaw power station in 1971 and the Ford engine plant at Bridgend in January 1980.

Having passed through the station at Gileston, 0-6-2T No 5690 heads a westbound rake of coal empties from Aberthaw power station near St Athan on 29 August 1962. In the background can be seen the chimneys of Aberthaw cement works. There were five stations on this line, Southerndown Road, Llantwit Major, Gileston, Aberthaw and Rhoose, halts being added later at Llandow and St Athan, both serving RAF camps. Passenger services were withdrawn on 15 July 1964, but the line survives today as a diversionary route for the South Wales main line. It reopened to regular passenger services in June 2005 with the introduction of a local service from Barry to Bridgend, calling at Rhoose and Llantwit Major.

This splendid picture taken in Barry Docks recalls the halcyon days of the steam era as 0-6-2T No 5658 heads trip working number 'J32' on 8 August 1962. Work on the docks at Barry, developed solely as a coal port by Welsh industrialist David Davies, commenced in 1884. The first dock basin opened in 1889, to be followed by two other docks and port installations. Trade grew from one million tons in the first year to more than 9 million tons by 1903, reaching a climax of 11 million tons a year by 1913. Behind the docks rise the terraced houses of Barry which together with Cadoxton soon formed a sizeable town.

LEFT The Waterhall Junction–Common Branch Junction line was sustained for many years by one morning trip working to Creigiau quarry. On 18 April 1964 an 0-6-0PT is seen propelling empties to the quarry. Opened in the 1870s, this dolomite pit supplied stone used in the construction of Cardiff Docks and later the lime/magnesium used for steelmaking at Guest-Keen's Tremorfa works.

RIGHT In 1964 the station at Creigiau still boasted an original dark-blue Barry Railway enamel sign, but today the old passenger platform survives only to serve an overgrowth of grass tussock, dogwood and ivy. For a short time the quarry did small-time road stone and material for river revetments until 2001 when costs outstripped prices and work ceased. This view depicts the 0-6-0PT shunting at the quarry.

LEFT Another picture of the same '94xx' 0-6-0PT on 18 April 1964 shows it passing the site of St Fagans Road siding. The Llantrisant Common branch ran from Llantrisant Common Junction (connecting with the GWR Ely branch) to Common Branch Junction. It opened on 1 December 1863 for freight and mineral traffic, but today only the disused rail bridges reveal where this line once cut across the old Llantrisant Common.

RIGHT With coal traffic passing through from a number of different valleys, Tondu was another important railway centre. In this view taken on 29 August 1962 an unidentified '42xx' 2-8-0T is seen passing Tondu Middle signalbox with coal empties. The line to the right leads to the Ogmore and Garw valleys, that to the left leading to the Llynfi valley; another line linked these two with the locomotive shed in the centre. Becoming 88H on 1 January 1961, the depot closed in April 1964, and the displaced locomotives were reallocated to 11 different depots. Today the locomotive shed has been demolished and only the running lines remain.

LEFT Also pictured at Tondu on 29 August 1962, 0-6-0PT No 3616 has arrived with a train from Blaengwynfi. Whilst the movement of coal was the main reason for railways in this area, a number of passenger services developed, both to the mining communities and the coast. At the time this photograph was taken the $2^{1}/_{2}$-mile Abergwynfi–Cymmer section had already closed; services on the Cymmer–Bridgend line were withdrawn in 1970, but passenger trains between Bridgend and Maesteg recommenced in September 1992. A long-time resident at Tondu MPD, No 3616 had subsequent allocations to Aberdare (88J), Neath (87A) and Gloucester Horton Rd (85B) before withdrawal in October 1965. Stored at Worcester (85A), the locomotive was broken up at Birds of Long Marston.

Photographed from the road which passed over the end of Crumlin Low Level station, an unidentified 0-6-0PT crosses the viaduct at Crumlin with a Neath–Pontypool Road train on 27 July 1963. A well-known feature in the Ebbw Valley, the viaduct was built between 1853 and 1857 by the Newport, Abergavenny & Hereford Railway, being constructed in two parts separated by a ridge of high ground.

ABOVE Demolition work on the huge iron and brick structure of Walnut Tree Viaduct was carried out between April and October 1969. In this picture, taken in September, one of the lattice girders has been lowered to the railway track below. Through services over the viaduct were withdrawn from 22 July 1963, freight services to the adjacent dolomite quarry continuing until the last train crossed the structure on 14 December 1967. Two piers were retained, one of which was decorated in 1977 to mark the Silver Jubilee of Queen Elizabeth II.

RIGHT Viewed from the road that follows the east side of the valley on 31 July 1963, the vast expanse of railway infrastructure that once served the Ebbw Valley is readily apparent. An 0-6-0PT heads a short freight up the valley past the former Llanhilleth Steam Coal Colliery, and to the left can be seen Llanhilleth Junction Middle signalbox. On the right the two tracks lead up to the single line which joined the Neath-Pontypool Road route at Crumlin Junction. That link, which was opened in 1855, never had a public passenger service but was used by workmen's trains from Brynmawr to ROF Glascoed until 24 April 1961.

Built for the GWR by the North British Locomotive Co in Glasgow, 0-6-0PT No 7754 worked in various areas of the GWR system until it was withdrawn from service at Wellington (84H) MPD in January 1959. After spending six months in store at Swindon Works it was sold to the National Coal Board in August 1959, and is seen here at NCB Tirphil on 4 June 1965. After subsequent operation at Talywain and Mountain Ash collieries, it was preserved in 1975 and is normally to be found in service on the Llangollen Railway.

0-6-2T No 5683 is seen on 3 June 1962 between Ystrad Mynach and Hengoed Low Level on the former Rhymney Railway main line, working a loaded coal train. The line to the right joined the Rhymney Railway to the Vale of Neath line, giving LNWR trains from the Sirhowy Valley access to Cardiff. The Rhymney Railway was built to carry coal from the Rhymney Valley to Cardiff. Initially it ran over the Taff Vale from Walnut Tree Junction, but congestion and difficulties with the Taff Vale caused the Rhymney to build its own direct line to Cardiff, this being completed in 1871.

LEFT After passing over the junction at Maesycymmer, down trains ran to Hengoed Viaduct and crossed over the Rhymney river, which was then the boundary between England and Wales. Here an unidentified 0-6-0PT heads a westbound goods over the viaduct on 31 May 1962. Frequently referred to as the Maesycymmer Viaduct (and in early references the Rhymney Viaduct), it stands at 298yd long on 16 stone arches, 130ft high and on a slight curve. Construction began in mid 1853 and it was the last major piece of the Taff Vale Extension (TVE) to be completed before opening in 1858. On the eastern side of the valley the Brecon & Merthyr main line passed under through a skewed arch, and a connection to it trailed in on the up side of the TVE at Maesycymmer Junction.

ABOVE Merthyr (88D) MPD's 0-6-0PT No 6416 is seen approaching the eastern portal of Merthyr Tunnel with a train for Hirwaun on 28 April 1962. No 6416 also had the dubious honour of working services on the last day of operation – 29 December 1962. Whereas the western portal was built to accommodate double track, the eastern portal was single-track only. Also known as Abernant Tunnel, this 2,497yd tunnel under Mynydd Gethin was one of the longest in the area. Lined in part with stone blocks, the roof of the tunnel was strongly engineered in brick, and at the centre of the tunnel were two enlarged workmen's recesses containing a fireplace and bench, designed for workers' breaks.

One of several 0-6-0PTs sold into NCB service to work in the South Wales valleys, No 9792 is seen at Maerdy Colliery on 31 March 1967. A long-term resident of Neath (87A) MPD, No 9792 was sold to the NCB in April 1964. After nationalisation the NCB spent £5 million completely reconstructing the colliery at Maerdy, including a new surface layout and a new horizon mining system underground. Also a link was made with the Bwllfa No 1 pit workings over two miles away at the head of the Dare valley. The last deep mine in the Rhondda valley, it effectively closed in 1985 when the last coal mined there was brought to the surface at Tower Colliery.

'NCB No 8' (RSH 7139 of 1944) is seen shunting internal wagons at Mountain Ash Colliery on 7 July 1962. In 1961 this locomotive had been rebuilt by the Hunslet Engine Co as its No 3880. Whilst it is common knowledge that Swindon built the last main-line steam locomotive, No 92220 *Evening Star*, it was in Leeds that British steam-locomotive construction finally ceased more than a decade later. The very last locomotive that was built for anything other than leisure, heritage or novelty value was demonstrated to the press a little over 40 years ago, on 26 November 1971.

This picture taken from the footbridge at Cresselly Crossing, Mountain Ash, on 31 May 1962 depicts Aberdare (86J) MPD's 0-6-0PT No 3753 on shunting duties. Although not visible, the footbridge passed over all three lines, but the level-crossing gates spanned only two; the third was a colliery track, the span of the footbridge over this line being of a different design.

Another view taken on 31 May 1962 near Cresselly Crossing depicts green-liveried 0-6-2T No 6651 as it propels a loaded coal train towards the crossing. One of 13 examples of this class allocated to Aberdare (88J) MPD at this time, No 6651 was reallocated to Pontypool Road (86G) in February 1963 but stayed only until May; in that month it was despatched to Croes Newydd (6C) MPD, from where it worked until withdrawn in October 1965. After storage until January 1966 at Croes Newydd, it was finally broken up at Cashmore's at Great Bridge. It was another Croes Newydd MPD locomotive, No 6697, which held the distinction of being the last member of the class in traffic, this engine now being preserved at the Didcot Railway Centre.

'57xx' 0-6-0PT No 3685 is seen crossing Joint Line Junction and arriving at Quakers Yard (High Level) station on a sunny 31 March 1962 with the 11.15am service from Aberdare (High Level) to Pontypool Road. With 11 intermediate stops, the train was allowed some 67 minutes to cover the 23 miles. Passengers from Merthyr Tydfil could connect with this service via the Low Level station. Whilst the Low Level station remains open today, High Level closed on 15 June 1964. No 3685, a long-time resident of Pontypool Road (86G) MPD, was withdrawn in April 1964 and subsequently despatched to Swindon Works for breaking up.

The view west at Maesycymmer Junction on 27 July 1963, as an 0-6-0PT threads its way through the points with a brake van. The lines dropping away sharply to the right of the picture join the Brecon & Merthyr at Fleur-de-Lis. The signalbox on the left, which had 31 levers, closed on 15 June 1964, together with the lines over the viaduct. The other routes continued in use until 20 November 1967, the only regular passenger service northwards being for Glascoed munition workers, which continued until 1963.

There were two stations at Pontllanfraith – High Level, on the Sirhowy Valley line, and Low Level, seen here as 0-6-2T No 5624 heads a Pontypool Road-Neath train on 27 July 1963. There was a triangle at Pontllanfraith which allowed trains from the LNWR and GWR to exchange traffic, being one of many complex junctions in the valleys. Within a matter of yards three junctions existed here – Sirhowy Junction, Tredegar Lower Junction and Bird-in-Hand Junction. Above the train the footbridge carries an advertisement for Hancocks Fine Beers. This company's brewing operations can be traced back to 1807, and by the 1870s it was the largest brewer in the West of England. In 1968 the company was acquired by the Bass Charrington Group, later becoming part of Welsh Brewers Ltd.

Between Taff Bargoed Junction and Cwmbargoed on the original Great Western and Rhymney joint line there were gradients between 1 in 40 and 1 in 49 for almost seven miles. At the end of the climb was the remote station at Cwmbargoed, seen here in September 1963 as 0-6-2T No 5660 departs with a train from Ystrad Mynach to Dowlais Cae Harris. To the left of the picture is the branch from Fochriw Colliery. The line remains open today for freight from Ffos-y-Fran opencast coal mine.

Opened in 1853, Abernant was the second intermediate station on the line between Merthyr and Gelli Tarw Junction. Captured on 31 May 1962 is 0-6-0PT No 6416 as it arrives with an auto-train shuttle service from Merthyr to Hirwaun. This provided a link between Merthyr Tydfil and the Pontypool Road-Neath line until services were withdrawn from 31 December 1962. The trackbed along this section of the Cynon Valley forms a footpath from Cwmbach to Llwydcoed for the use of walkers, ramblers and other leisure users.

On the same day this train was seen again, this time at Llwydcoed. The station here had no sidings, and was in use throughout the life of the line. Whilst work on the line had commenced in 1847, the 2,495yd Merthyr Tunnel took until August 1853 to complete. Before the tunnel was completed a temporary station called Merthyr Road was used, Llwydcoed being the only intermediate station when the route first opened.

LEFT Another view at Llwydcoed, this time taken from the road overbridge shows more detail of the station building as an auto-train from Hirwaun departs for Merthyr on 7 July 1962. Today the site of the station is overgrown, although the platform formation is still *in situ*, the adjacent Station House and nearby Station Villas providing a reminder of their railway origins.

ABOVE On 30 June 1962 Pontypool Road (86G) MPD's 0-6-0PT No 3708 is seen arriving at Nelson & Llancaiach with a train from Aberdare. The one-mile Penalltau Junction–Nelson & Llancaiach section of the former Vale of Neath line proved to be the busiest, with over 50 trains a day in each direction immediately before World War 1. At Penalltau the Rhymney Railway headed south towards Ystrad Mynach and Cardiff. This important link opened in 1871, with through running powers granted by the GWR, giving the RR a major new source of traffic.

This March 1973 view sees 0-6-0ST *Sir Gomer* passing light-engine over the River Taff at Mountain Ash Colliery. Named after Sir James Gomer Berry, the newspaper proprietor and industrial magnate, it was built by Peckett & Sons in 1932 and delivered to the Mountain Ash Colliery of Llewellyn (Nixon) Ltd, becoming the property of Powell Duffryn Associated Collieries in 1936. Upon nationalisation of the coal industry in 1947 it became the property of the NCB, and after spending its whole working life at Mountain Ash it was retired in 1981.

The steelworks at Llanelly opened its doors in 1907 and quickly became known to the local population as 'Klondike'. Whilst the pay was good the conditions were primitive, men and boys working alongside each other in a hot, oppressive atmosphere in which injury and even death were commonplace. Things improved in 1960 when the works was bought by Canadian-based Duport Steel, but after financial difficulties some 20 years later production ended in 1981, and the site was abandoned. Here Peckett No 2159/1955 is seen shunting outside the melting shop on 10 June 1967. Built for use at the Barrow Ironworks in Lancashire, it was transferred to Llanelly in August 1964 and remained in operation until 1969.

Against a backdrop of the winding gear at Caerau Colliery in the Llynfi valley, Hunslet 0-6-0ST No 2867 *Patricia* makes its way into the yard on 21 March 1967. The South and North pits were sunk in 1883, reaching a depth of 1,020ft, being followed by a third shaft, sunk in 1909, which found house-coal seams at a depth of 516ft. In the ownership of Lord Rhondda the colliery employed 4,104 men and in 1935 helped produce one million tons of coal alongside Coegnant, Maesteg. By 1961 the workforce was down to 641 and output 122,244 tons, closure coming 16 years later, in 1977.

Neath (87A) MPD's 0-6-0PT No 4621 is seen arriving at Devynock & Sennybridge with a Neath-Brecon train on 23 June 1962. The Neath & Brecon Railway was established to build a standard-gauge line connecting the collieries in the Dulais valley with the then broad-gauge Vale of Neath Railway at Cadoxton, giving access to Neath and Swansea docks. The line was absorbed into the GWR in July 1922 as part of the Grouping, but only after the LMS withdrew its through Hereford-Swansea trains, in December 1930, did the GWR introduce Brecon-Neath trains. Along with all other lines to Brecon, the northern section closed in December 1962.

A general view of the shed yard, looking north, at Duffryn Yard (87B) MPD in 1961, with the Maesteg line going away to the right. Built by the Port Talbot Railway in 1896 as a five-road straight shed, the depot was partially reconstructed by the GWR in 1931, when a sixth track was added along with a larger turntable and more efficient coaling facilities. Concerned primarily with providing motive power for freight traffic but also for some passenger services, it was demolished shortly after closure on 2 March 1964.